ARM KNITTING

How to Make a 30-Minute Infinity Scarf and Other Great Projects

Mary Beth Temple

Contents

Simple Infinity
Scarf 18

Chunky
Mobius 20

Striped
Hooded Scarf 22

Fringed Knotted
Stitch Scarf. 24

Magenta Medley
Scarf 26

Button-Up
Cowl 28

Duet Cowl. 30

Color Block
Infinity Scarf 32

Color Block
Wrap. 34

Ombré Scarf. 36

Neon Braid
Scarf 38

Striped Knotted
Stitch Capelet 40

Two Layer
Cape 42

One Point
Wrap. 44

Shaped
Shawl 46

About Metric

Throughout this book, you'll notice that every measurement is accompanied by a metric equivalent. Inches and feet are rounded off to the nearest half or whole centimeter unless precision is necessary (note that some larger measurements are rounded off to the nearest meter). Please be aware that while this book will show 1 yard = 100 centimeters, the actual conversion is 1 yard = 90 centimeters, a difference of about 3 15⁄16" (10cm). Using these conversions, you will always have a little bit of extra yarn if measuring using the metric system.

Getting Started

If you have a few skeins of yarn on hand, you are ready to get started with arm knitting! In this section, you'll find everything you need to make the classic infinity scarf in three different stitches. Once you get comfortable with the basics, learn how to take your projects to the next level with techniques for color work, adding embellishments, and more!

Casting On

When working arm knitting projects, always use the yarn from the outside of the skein, even if it's a center-pull ball, so the yarn does not become knotted as you're working.

In arm knitting, you almost always work more than one strand at a time, and each strand is taken from its own skein. Hold the strands together and treat them as one as you work. The photos here show three strands being treated as one.

Tip

When casting on, it is always better to have too much tail yarn than too little. When in doubt, leave a long tail when casting on so you never have to worry about running out!

1| Prepare the strands. To work with three strands, start with three skeins of yarn. Pull a strand from the outside of each skein and even up the ends.

2| Start the slip knot. Measure in 1–2 yd. (100–200cm) from the ends of the strands and form a slip knot. Start by forming a loop with the strands. Then twist it so the strands cross at the bottom.

3| Complete the slip knot.
Reach through the loop, grab the top set of strands, and pull it through, forming a new loop. Tighten the knot by gently tugging on the loose ends. Slide the loop of the slip knot onto your right wrist and tighten it slightly. Keep the loop loose enough to slide up and down your arm as you work.

4| Prepare the strands. The set of strands attached to the skeins is the working yarn and the set of strands hanging loose is the tail. Position the working yarn farthest from you and the tail closest to you. Insert your left thumb and index finger between the two sets of strands and spread your fingers apart.

5| Form a V. Pull the slip knot down over your palm between your thumb and forefinger, forming a V shape with the yarn. Grasp the loose strands with the remaining fingers of your left hand.

6| Go through the first loop.
Holding the yarn strands in place on your left hand, insert your right hand through the loop on your left hand that is closest to you (the one around your thumb). Put your hand through the loop from front to back, going away from your body.

7| Go through the second loop. Insert your right hand through the loop on your left index finger from back to front, going toward your body. Push this loop up on your wrist and let go of the strands in your left hand

8| Finish the second stitch.
Tighten the loop slightly by tugging gently on the tail end. You now have two stitches on your right arm (the slip knot counts as the first stitch). Repeat steps 4–8 to cast on the number of stitches indicated for your desired pattern.

Arm Knitting

Plain Stitch

This is the classic stitch used for arm knitting. It will create a smooth side and a knotted side to your project. To start, cast on the indicated number of stitches to your right arm.

1| Loop the yarn. Take the working yarn and loop it over your right thumb from front to back (away from your body). Grasp the working yarn with the fingers of your right hand to hold it in place around your thumb.

2| Pull off a stitch. Pull the first loop on your right arm (the one closest to your hand) over your right hand and let it go. Continue to hold the working yarn in place on your right thumb.

Tip

Starting each stitch by wrapping the yarn around your thumb is a great way to learn and remember where the working yarn should be positioned as you work. Once you understand this, you will no longer need to wrap the working yarn around your thumb to position it properly.

3| Transfer the loop. Transfer the loop on your right thumb to your left arm, twisting the loop clockwise to bring the working yarn close to you. Tighten the loop slightly by gently tugging on the working yarn. Repeat steps 1–3 to move all the stitches from your right arm to your left. This completes the first row.

4| Make the second row. To make a second row, use the same method to transfer the stitches from your left arm to your right. Twist the loops counterclockwise when transferring them to bring the working yarn close to you. Repeat until you have moved all the stitches from your right arm to your left. This completes the second row.

Tip

In Plain Stitch, the plain, smooth side of the work (the loop side) always faces toward you, while the knotted side always faces away from you.

Twisted Stitch

If you're looking for something a little more decorative than Plain Stitch, Twisted Stitch is for you. This technique causes the "legs" of each stitch to cross, creating a very pretty effect that is simple to achieve. This method will make slightly tighter stitches, so there will be less open space in your finished project. To start, cast on the indicated number of stitches to your right arm.

1| Loop the yarn. Take the working yarn and loop it over your right thumb from back to front (toward your body). Grasp the working yarn with the fingers of your right hand to hold it in place around your thumb.

2| Pull off a stitch. Pull the first loop on your right arm (the one closest to your hand) over your right hand and let it go. Continue to hold the working yarn in place on your right thumb.

3| Transfer the loop. Transfer the loop on your right thumb to your left arm. Do not twist the loop as you did with Plain Stitch. This will keep the working yarn close to you. Tighten the loop slightly by gently tugging on the working yarn. Repeat steps 1–3 to move all the stitches from your right arm to your left. This completes the first row.

4| Make the second row. To make a second row use the same method to transfer the stitches from your left arm to your right. Do not twist the loops; this will keep the working yarn close to you. Repeat until you have moved all the stitches from your left arm to your right. This completes the second row.

Tip

In Twisted Stitch, the knotted side of the work always faces you, while the plain, smooth side of the work (the loop side) always faces away from you. You will see the "legs" of the stitches on the smooth side cross, adding a decorative touch.

Plain Stitch

Twisted Stitch

Knotted Stitch

Knotted Stitch is simply a combination of Plain Stitch and Twisted Stitch. Using Knotted Stitch, your finished project will look the same on both sides, with alternating rows of knots and loops. To start, cast on the indicated number of stitches to your right arm. Work the first row in Plain Stitch, moving the stitches from your right arm to your left. Work the second row in Twisted Stitch, moving the stitches from your left arm to your right. Continue alternating rows of Plain Stitch and Twisted Stitch for the length of your project.

Binding Off

Binding off finishes the edge of your project and allows you to take it off your arm! You can bind off working from your left arm to your right or your right arm to your left; the process is the same. The photos below illustrate binding off from left to right.

1| Make two stitches.
Work two stitches in the pattern you have been using for your project (e.g., Plain Stitch, Twisted Stitch, or Knotted Stitch). If working from left to right as shown, you will have two stitches on your right arm.

2| Take off the first stitch.
Take the first stitch (the one farthest from your hand on your right arm) and bring it over the second stitch and your hand. Let it go. You will be left with one stitch on your arm.

3| Make a stitch. Work one stitch in the pattern you have been using for your project. You will have two stitches on your right arm.

4| Take off the first stitch.
Repeat step 2, bringing the first stitch over the second stitch and your hand, leaving one stitch on your arm. Repeat steps 3–4 until you are left with one stitch on your right arm.

5| Trim the yarn. When you are down to one stitch, trim the working yarn so you have an 8"–10" (20.5 x 25.5cm) tail. If you intend to seam your scarf, leave a longer bind-off tail.

6| Pull the tail through.
Grab the tail with your right hand and pull it through the final stitch. Tug on the tail to tighten the knot.

Seaming

Seaming connects the ends of your project to create a continuous piece, like an infinity scarf or cowl. It is best to work on a flat surface, such as a table, for this technique. When seaming, remember the stitches you are weaving through have two loops. As you weave the bind-off tail through the stitches, make sure you are passing them under both loops of each stitch and not just one.

1| Align the edges. Place the short ends of your scarf against each other, making sure the scarf is not twisted.

2| Pick up the first two stitches. Start at the bottom edge. Working from right to left, feed your fingers through the first stitch of the right end of the scarf and the first stitch of the left end of the scarf. These stitches will be opposite one another.

3| Pull the tail through. Pull the bind-off tail through the two stitches you have on your fingers from left to right. Tug gently on the bind-off tail to tighten it, but do not pull it so tight that you cause the seam to pucker.

4| Work the remaining stitches. Repeat steps 2–3 with the next set of stitches. Feed your fingers through from right to left, and then pull the bind-off tail through from left to right. Repeat with the remaining stitches.

5| Finish the end. After feeding the bind-off tail through the last set of stitches, tie the tail into an overhand knot over a strand from the stitches and weave in the ends (see page 10).

Tip

If you'd like to make a Mobius scarf (a scarf with a twist in it), before seaming, bring the short ends of your scarf together with a 180° twist in the scarf. If you worked in Plain Stitch or Twisted Stitch, when you twist the scarf, at one end you will see the smooth side, and at the other end you will see the knotted side.

Weaving In Ends

When you finish a project, you will have some loose ends of yarn attached to it from your cast-on and bind-off tails, or perhaps from switching colors. These ends can be woven into the stitches of your project to hide them and to give your piece a clean, finished look.

1| Thread a strand. Thread one of the loose ends you need to weave in onto a tapestry needle.

2| Pass through the knot. If there is a knot at the base of the end you are weaving in, use the needle to bring the loose end through the knot, going from the outer edge of the piece toward the inside.

3| Split the plies. Follow the end you need to weave in back into the work and find a stitch near the edge that has a strand of the same color. Use the tip of the needle to split the plies of the stitch strand and bring the loose end through them.

4| Work for several inches. Weave the loose end through the plies of the stitch strand for several inches. Then, trim the loose end close to the stitch strand.

5| Weave in the remaining ends. Repeat steps 1–4 with the remaining loose ends. It is important to weave each loose end into a different stitch strand. Do not weave multiple ends into the same stitch strand. When you are finished, you will have a seamless piece with no loose ends dangling from it!

Vertical Stripes

This technique allows you to create a project with two colors, side by side, without having to make pieces in each color and stitch them together. For color stripes with an even width, cast on an odd number of stitches in two different colors as described below. You can alter the width of the stripes by casting on more or fewer stitches in each color.

1| Cast on. Cast on an odd number of stitches in two different colors. These photos show five light blue stitches and four dark blue stitches (nine total). You will have two tails and two sets of working yarn. The tails shown are cut very short. Make sure you leave a long tail when you make your project.

2| Work the first set of stitches. Work all the stitches before the center stitch in your chosen pattern. Use the working yarn in the color that matches the loops you are moving.

3| Work the center stitch. Use both sets of working yarn, instead of just one, to work the center stitch (in this case, stitch five). Do not tighten the center stitch as much as the others; it will naturally be tighter because it has twice as many strands.

4| Work the second set of stitches. Work all the stitches after the center stitch in your chosen pattern. Use the working yarn in the color that matches the loops you are moving.

5| Repeat. Continue this pattern for the length of your project. In each row, the first set of stitches will be in one color, the center stitch will be two-tone, and the last set of stitches will be in the second color. This creates vertical stripes in two colors the length of your project.

Horizontal Stripes

Using this technique, you can create alternating horizontal stripes every two rows without leaving multiple ends that need to be woven in once you finish the project. This results in a heavier stitch on one edge of the piece, so it should be incorporated into your design as an edging. This technique is perfect for wraps or capelets where you might want to finish one edge differently than the other.

1| Stitch the first two rows.
Cast on the indicated number of stitches in one color. Work a row in that color until only one stitch remains on your right arm. On the last stitch, pick up a set of strands in your second color and carry it through the stitch with the working yarn in the first color. This creates a two-tone stitch. Make sure you leave a very long tail on the color you have added (at least 12" [30.5cm]).

2| Stitch the next two rows.
Work the third row, using both sets of working yarn on the two-tone stitch. Then use the working yarn in the second color for the remaining stitches in the row. Work the fourth row in the second color.

3| Repeat. Continue the pattern, alternating colors every two rows, and always carrying both sets of working yarn through the two-tone stitch. Note: When moving loops from right to left, the two-tone stitch will be the last stitch you make. When moving loops from left to right, the two-tone stitch will be the first stitch.

Tip

Just like the center stitch in the vertical stripe pattern, the two-tone stitch in this pattern will be tighter than the other stitches because it is made up of more strands. Don't tighten the two-tone stitches too much, or your work will pucker along the edge.

Color Blocking

This technique allows you to stitch multiple rows in one color and then switch to another color. To start, cast on the indicated number of stitches in your first color and work the desired number of rows.

1| Work the first color. Work the desired number of rows in your first color. When you are ready to switch to a new color, trim the working yarn of the color you're using, leaving an 8"–10" (20.5 x 25.5cm) tail. Snug up all stitches.

2| Tie on the second color. Align the working yarn of the first color with a set of strands in the second color. Use the two sets of strands to tie an overhand knot as close to the edge of your work as possible.

3| Work the second color. Work the desired number of rows using the new color you just added. Switch colors again as desired using this technique. When the project reaches the desired length, weave in the ends of all the loose strands where you switched colors.

Increasing

Increasing allows you to add stitches to rows so you can make a project wider. The technique is the same no matter which stitch you are using. Increasing can be done at the beginning of a row on either edge of your project, but not at the end of a row. You can also increase in the middle of a row. Increasing can be done with the stitches on either arm; the process is the same.

1| Prepare the strands. Bring the working yarn around your thumb in the manner described for the stitch you are using. Insert your fingers between the first and second loop on your arm.

2| Pull the working yarn through. Pull the working yarn through the space between the first and second loops. Release the working yarn from your thumb as you pull it through. Place the resulting loop on your wrist with the other loops. Work the next row, starting with the increase stitch you just made. You have increased the stitches in the row by one.

Decreasing

Decreasing allows you to remove stitches from rows so you can make a project narrower. The technique is the same no matter which stitch you are using. Decreasing can be done anywhere in a row, as it basically turns two stitches into one. Decreasing can be done with the stitches on either arm; the process is the same.

1| Pick up two stitches. Bring the working yarn around your thumb in the manner described for the stitch you are using. Pick up the first two stitches on your arm.

2| Pull off the stitches. Pull the two stitches over your hand and let them go. Place the loop around your thumb on the opposite hand in the manner described for the stitch you are using. Work the remaining stitches in the row as usual. You have decreased the stitches in the row by one.

Aligning Patterned Yarn

Some yarns come in a striped pattern, making it super easy for you to create a striped scarf! Not every skein of patterned yarn starts at the same place in the pattern, however. Because arm knitting uses multiple skeins of yarn at once, it's important that you align your patterned yarn before you get started to make sure your stripes come out as you intended!

1| Check the ends. Start with the number of skeins required for your project. Pull out a strand of yarn from each skein and align the ends to see if they start at the same place in the pattern.

2| Align the pattern. If the ends do not start at the same place in the pattern, continue to pull out lengths of yarn from each skein until you can match them up at a point where the pattern aligns. Trim the yarn at your new starting point.

Finishing a Neckline

Cut some extra lengths of yarn after binding off and use them to finish the neckline of a stunning cape or capelet! The process is very similar to seaming.

1| Weave through the first stitch. Turn the project so the wrong side is facing you. Make sure the short edges are positioned vertically to your right and left. Feed your fingers through the first stitch of the top edge from front to back. Grab the neckline strands and pull them through the stitch from back to front.

2| Weave through the second stitch. Feed your fingers through the next stitch from back to front and pull the neckline strands through from front to back. Continue weaving the neckline strands in and out of the stitches along the top edge of the work.

3| Finish. Slide stitches along neckline strands until the top edge measures the length indicated for your project. Finish both ends of the neckline by tying the strands together in an overhand knot over the end stitches. Weave in the ends as shown on page 10.

Tip

The stitches you are weaving through have two loops. As you weave the neckline strands through the stitches, make sure you are passing them under *both* loops of each stitch and not just one.

Fringe

Adding fringe is a great way to put a decorative touch on the ends of a scarf you do not want to seam and turn into an infinity scarf. Add fringe using the same yarn you did for your project, or change it up by using a different color or different yarn altogether!

1| Prepare the strands.
Cut several strands of yarn for each fringe. Make the strands twice as long as the desired length of the fringe, plus 2" (5cm). It's always better to make the strands too long than too short; you can always trim the fringe back later. Fold the strands in half to form a loop at the center.

2| Thread the loop. Feed the loop through one of the stitches at the end of your project.

3| Thread the ends. Bring the ends of the fringe through the loop and tug on them gently to tighten the knot.

4| Fringe any loose ends.
Incorporate the tails from binding off or casting on in your fringe. When you reach the stitch next to the cast-on or bind-off tail, pull the tail through the loop with the ends of the fringe. Trim all fringe evenly.

Pom-Pom

Pom-poms can be used to add a fun touch to any project! Add small ones anywhere in the project for decoration, or fill the ends of your scarf with big fluffy ones for a playful look.

1| Prepare the cardboard.
Cut a piece of cardboard with a width equal to half the desired diameter of the finished pom-pom; the height does not matter. Cut a 12"–15" (30.5 x 38cm) length of yarn to tie your pom-pom. Place the yarn lengthwise in the center of the cardboard.

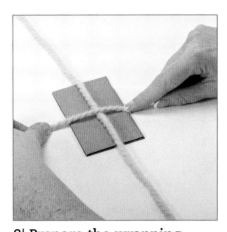

2| Prepare the wrapping strand. Pull a strand of yarn from a skein and place it widthwise in the center of the cardboard, over the first yarn strand. Align the end of the wrapping strand with the edge of the cardboard.

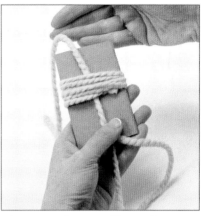

3| Wrap the cardboard.
Wrap the yarn strand attached to the skein around the cardboard widthwise as many times as desired. The more wraps you make, the fuller your pom-pom will be. Let the ends of the 12"–15" (30.5 x 38cm) strand of yarn hang loose as you wrap.

4| Tie the pom-pom.
Once you've wrapped the cardboard as many times as desired, take the ends of the 12"–15" (30.5 x 38cm) strand and use them to tie a square knot over the wraps. Make the knot as tight as possible. Trim the end of the wrapping strand from the skein.

5| Cut the wraps.
Remove the cardboard, keeping the wraps in place around your fingers. Cut the wraps apart using scissors. Sharp scissors will help you cut through the yarn easily, but make sure you use caution so you don't cut your fingers.

6| Trim the ends.
Trim the ends of the pom-pom even for a uniform look. The shorter you cut the strands, the stiffer the pom-pom will be. For a more floppy pom-pom, leave the ends a bit longer. Use the tails from the square knot to tie the pom-pom onto your project.

Simple Infinity Scarf

This is the scarf that started it all. Following this simple pattern, you can create tons of different looks just by changing the yarn you use or the way you wear the finished piece. And it's so easy!

DIFFICULTY:

APPROXIMATE CIRCUMFERENCE:
56" (142cm)

STRANDS:
Use 3 strands held together throughout

MATERIALS:
- 3 skeins bulky weight yarn, 1 color

Scarf

1. Using 3 strands held together, cast on 12 stitches.

2. Work in Twisted Stitch for 25 rows or until work measures 56" (142cm) or desired length. Bind off.

3. Seam short ends together without a twist. Weave in ends.

Tip

Need to take a break, but not quite finished with your project? Complete a row, and then transfer the loops from your arm to a broom, yardstick, dowel, or similar item. When you're ready to start knitting again, simply transfer the loops back to your arm and start stitching!

Yarn
The project shown uses Lion Brand® Yarn Homespun® (6oz./185yd. [170g/169m]), 3 skeins #404 Lagoon.

Chunky Mobius

Put a twist on the classic infinity scarf by sewing it into a Mobius (a circle with a 180° twist in it)! Seaming the scarf with a twist in it will show off both the knotted and the smooth side of the Plain Stitch, giving you a finished piece that's full of texture.

DIFFICULTY:

APPROXIMATE CIRCUMFERENCE:
32" (81cm)

STRANDS:
Use 5 strands held together throughout, 4 of Color A, 1 of Color B

MATERIALS:
- 2 skeins (divided) super bulky weight yarn, 1 color
- 1 skein sport weight yarn, 1 color

Mobius

1. Using 5 strands held together (4 strands Color A and 1 strand Color B), cast on 12 stitches.

2. Work in Plain Stitch for 15 rows or until work measures 32" (81cm) or desired length. Bind off.

3. Sew into a Mobius shape by twisting one short end 180° before seaming as shown on page 9. Weave in ends.

Tip
Because this project is so short, you only need to buy two skeins of Color A. Divide both skeins into two even balls.

Yarn
The project shown uses Lion Brand® Yarn Wool-Ease® Thick & Quick® (6oz./106yd. [170g/97m]), 2 skeins (divided) #104 Pine (Color A) and Lion Brand® Yarn Vanna's Glamour® (1.75oz./202yd. [50g/185m]), 1 skein #100 Diamond (Color B).

Striped Hooded Scarf

Use yarn with a stripe pattern to create this fun color block hoodie. You won't have to change colors or patterns because the yarn does it for you! Adding a seam at the center of the scarf creates a hood, making this an extra cozy piece to wear.

DIFFICULTY:

APPROXIMATE LENGTH:
80" (203cm)

STRANDS:
Use 3 strands held together throughout

MATERIALS:
- 3 skeins super bulky weight yarn, 1 color in stripe pattern

Hoodie

1. Line up yarn strands to keep stripe pattern even throughout, as shown on page 14.

2. Using 3 strands held together, cast on 7 stitches.

3. Work in Plain Stitch until 7 color blocks have been completed or until work measures 80" (203cm) or desired length. Bind off.

4. Fold scarf in half with knotted sides facing. Sew seam for hood from fold down 11" (28cm).

5. Weave in ends.

Yarn
The project shown uses Lion Brand® Yarn Wool-Ease® Thick & Quick® Stripes (5oz./87yd. [140g/80m]), 3 skeins #604 Huskies.

Fringed Knotted Stitch Scarf

Change up the appearance of your arm knitting by working in Knotted Stitch to create a piece with lots of eye-catching texture. Adding fringe to the ends leaves you with no finishing to do and no seams to sew!

DIFFICULTY:

APPROXIMATE LENGTH:
100" (254cm), including fringe

STRANDS:
Use 6 strands held together throughout, 2 of each color

MATERIALS:
- 6 skeins super bulky weight yarn, 3 colors, 2 skeins each color

Scarf

1. Using 6 strands held together (2 strands each color), cast on 5 stitches, leaving a tail at least 16" (40.5cm) long.

2. Work in Knotted Stitch for 36 rows or until work measures 70" (178cm) or desired length. Bind off, leaving a tail at least 16" (40.5cm) long.

Yarn
The project shown uses Lion Brand® Yarn Hometown USA® (5oz./81yd. [142g/74m]), 2 skeins each #113 Cincinnati Red, #009 Los Angeles Tan, and Lion Brand® Yarn Hometown USA® (4oz./64yd. [113g/59m]), 2 skeins #208 Phoenix Azalea.

Fringe

1. Cut 20 strands of each color 32" (81cm) long. Work fringe as shown on page 16 using 6 strands (2 strands each color) for each fringe, incorporating the cast-on/bind-off tails as shown on page 16.

2. Trim fringe evenly.

Magenta Medley Scarf

Your arm knitting pieces don't have to be chunky to be fashionable! If you're looking for something with a little less bulk, try using lighter weight yarns to create thinner projects. Faux fur and eyelash yarns, or those with a little sparkle woven in, are perfect for making dressier projects. Try finishing the ends with beads!

DIFFICULTY:

APPROXIMATE LENGTH:
152" (386cm), including tails

STRANDS:
Use 3 strands held together throughout, 1 of each yarn type

MATERIALS:
- 1 skein bulky weight yarn, 1 color eyelash or fur texture
- 1 skein sport weight yarn, 1 color
- 1 skein worsted weight yarn, 1 color
- 6 silver mesh barrel beads (⅝" [16mm])

Yarn
The project shown uses Lion Brand® Yarn Fun Fur® (1.75oz./64yd. [50g/58m]), 1 skein #146 Magenta; Lion Brand® Yarn Vanna's Glamour® (1.75oz./202yd. [50g/185m]), 1 skein #146 Jewel; and Lion Brand® Yarn Vanna's Choice® (3.5oz./170yd. [100g/156m]), 1 skein #144 Magenta.

Scarf

1. Using 1 strand of each yarn type held together (3 strands total), cast on 3 stitches, leaving a long tail for the beads.

2. Work in Plain Stitch until work measures 142" (360.5) or desired length. Bind off, leaving a long tail for the beads.

Beading

1. Pull tails tight. Thread 3 beads onto each tail, tying a double overhand knot after each bead. Trim tails to 5" (12.5cm). Tie an overhand knot at the end of each tail strand to prevent fraying.

Button-Up Cowl

Incorporating buttons gives this piece a fun and funky flair. And there's no need to worry about sewing buttonholes—the large stitches used to make this piece will work just fine. This is literally a 15-minute project!

DIFFICULTY:

APPROXIMATE CIRCUMFERENCE:
27" (68.5cm), buttoned

STRANDS:
Use 5 strands held together throughout, 3 of Color A, 2 of Color B

MATERIALS:
- 2 skeins (1 divided) bulky weight yarn, 1 color (Color A)
- 1 skein (divided) super bulky weight yarn, 1 color (Color B)
- 3 buttons (1¾" [4.5cm])
- Sewing needle and coordinating thread

Cowl

1. Using 5 strands held together (3 strands Color A and 2 strands Color B), cast on 7 stitches.

2. Work in Plain Stitch for 13 rows or until work measures 27" (68.5cm) or desired length. Bind off.

3. Weave in ends.

4. Sew 3 buttons evenly spaced across one short end.

Tip
Because this project is so short, you only need to buy two skeins of Color A and one skein of Color B. Divide one A skein and the B skein into two even balls.

Alternative Closure
Don't feel like sewing on buttons? Use a pretty jewelry piece or a decorative shawl stick as a closure instead.

Yarn
The project shown uses Lion Brand® Yarn Homespun® (6oz./185yd. [170g/169m]), 2 skeins (1 divided) #315 Tudor (Color A); Lion Brand® Yarn Wool-Ease® Thick & Quick® (6oz./106yd. [170g/97m]), 1 skein (divided) #146 Fig (Color B); and La Mode 1¾" (4.5cm) buttons, style #48179.

Duet Cowl

Two tweedy shades of natural colors produce a chunky rustic look perfect for your favorite weekend jaunt. This piece is extra thick and cozy. Wear it wrapped around your shoulders or pull one edge up over your head to act as a hood.

DIFFICULTY: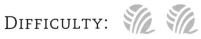

APPROXIMATE CIRCUMFERENCE:
64" (162.5cm)

STRANDS:
Use 3 strands held together throughout

MATERIALS:
- 6 skeins super bulky weight yarn, 2 colors, 3 skeins each color

Cowl

Using 3 strands held together, cast on 7 Color A and 8 Color B stitches (15 stitches).

Row 1: Work in Twisted Stitch here and throughout. Work 7 stitches Color B, 1 stitch Color B and Color A held together (see page 11), and 7 stitches Color A.

Row 2: Work 7 stitches Color A, 1 stitch Color A and Color B held together, and 7 stitches Color B.

Repeat Rows 1 and 2 for pattern until 34 rows have been completed or until work measures 64" (162.5cm) or desired length. Bind off.

Seam short ends together without a twist. Weave in ends.

Yarn

The project shown uses Lion Brand® Yarn Wool-Ease® Thick & Quick® (6oz./106yd. [170g/97m]), 3 skeins each #501 Sequoia (Color A), #123 Oatmeal (Color B).

Color Block Infinity Scarf

Stitch blocks of color together to create a fashionable look that is right on trend. Experiment with different color palettes for a totally new look every time! Try a classic neutral palette using creams and grays, or go all out with neon colors.

DIFFICULTY:

APPROXIMATE CIRCUMFERENCE:
72" (183cm)

STRANDS:
Use 3 strands held together throughout

MATERIALS:
- 9 skeins bulky weight yarn, 3 colors, 3 skeins each color

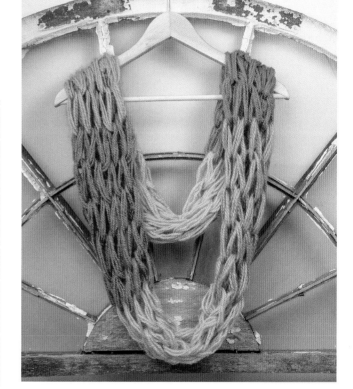

Counting Rows

When counting rows in a project, remember that the cast-on stitches count as a row, as does the row on your arm at the time you're counting!

Scarf

1. Using 3 strands of Color A held together, cast on 10 stitches.

2. Working in Plain Stitch throughout, work 4 more rows with Color A. Then work 5 rows each Color B, Color C, Color A, Color B, and Color C, changing colors using the Color Blocking technique shown on page 13. Bind off.

3. Seam short ends together without a twist. Weave in ends.

Yarn
The project shown uses Lion Brand® Yarn Jiffy® (3oz./135yd. [85g/123m]), 3 skeins each #103 Blossom (Color A), #195 Dusty Pink (Color B), #132 Apple Green (Color C).

Color Block Wrap

Take color blocking to a whole new level with this tri-color wrap. Fun fringe makes it extra cozy, while the neutral colors used for two of the blocks make the neon block really stand out. This piece is sure to become your go-to showstopper!

DIFFICULTY:

APPROXIMATE LENGTH:
92" (233.5cm), including fringe

APPROXIMATE WIDTH:
15" (38cm)

STRANDS:
Use 5 strands held together throughout

MATERIALS:
• 9 skeins super bulky weight yarn, 3 colors, 5 skeins Color A, 1 skein (divided) Color B, 3 skeins (2 divided) Color C

Tip

Because this project does not use a lot of Colors B and C, you only need to buy one skein of Color B and three skeins of Color C. Divide the B skein into five even balls. Divide two of the C skeins into two even balls each.

Counting Rows

When counting rows in a project, remember that the cast-on stitches count as a row, as does the row on your arm at the time you're counting!

Wrap

1. Using 5 strands of Color A held together, cast on 12 stitches, leaving a tail at least 16" (40.5cm) long.

2. Work in Plain Stitch for 18 rows total.

3. Change to 5 strands of Color B (see page 13). Work in Plain Stitch for 4 rows.

4. Change to 5 strands of Color C. Work in Plain Stitch for 8 rows.

5. Bind off using Color C, leaving a tail at least 16" (40.5cm) long.

Fringe

1. Cut 60 strands of each Color A and Color C 32" (81cm) long. Work fringe along each short end as shown on page 16, using 5 strands at a time. Match the color of the fringe to the color of the end you are working on. Incorporate the cast-on/bind-off tails as shown on page 16.

2. Trim fringe evenly to approximately 15" (38cm).

Yarn

The project shown uses Lion Brand® Yarn Hometown USA® (5oz./81yd. [142g/74m]), 5 skeins #149 Dallas Grey (Color A), 1 skein (divided) #400S Neon Pink (Color B), 3 skeins (2 divided) #999 Fisherman (Color C).

Ombré Scarf

Use varying shades of the same color to create a unique ombré look that will give your scarf the appearance of a hand-dyed masterpiece. Follow the color changes carefully to achieve the perfect transition between each shade!

DIFFICULTY: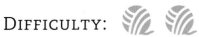

APPROXIMATE LENGTH:
80" (203cm)

STRANDS:
Use 6 strands held together throughout

MATERIALS:
- 3 skeins (divided) worsted weight yarn, 3 colors, 1 skein each color

Tip
Because this project does not require a lot of yarn, you only need to buy one skein of each color. Divide each skein into six even balls.

Counting Rows
When counting rows in a project, remember that the cast-on stitches count as a row, as does the row on your arm at the time you're counting!

Scarf

Using 6 strands of Color A held together, cast on 7 stitches.

Work in Plain Stitch for 35 rows total, following color sequence below. Change colors using the Color Blocking technique on page 13.

1. Work 4 more rows using 6 strands of Color A (5 rows total).

2. Work 5 rows using 4 strands of Color A + 2 strands of Color B.

3. Work 5 rows using 2 strands of Color A + 4 strands of Color B.

4. Work 5 rows using 6 strands of Color B.

5. Work 5 rows using 4 strands of Color B + 2 strands of Color C.

6. Work 5 rows using 2 strands of Color B + 4 strands of Color C.

7. Work 5 rows using 6 strands of Color C.

Bind off using Color C. Weave in ends.

Yarn

The project shown uses Lion Brand® Yarn Vanna's Choice® (3.5oz./170yd. [100g/156m]), 1 skein each (divided) #147 Purple (Color A), #145 Eggplant (Color B), #146 Dusty Purple (Color C).

Neon Braid Scarf

Nothing makes a neon color pop like pairing it with a neutral! The addition of pom-poms gives this trendy piece a fun and playful look that you'll love to show off.

DIFFICULTY: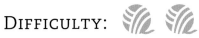

APPROXIMATE LENGTH:
100" (254cm), including pom-poms

STRANDS:
Use 3 strands held together throughout

MATERIALS:
- 9 skeins super bulky weight yarn, 3 colors, 3 skeins each color

Scarf

PLAIN STITCH STRIP
Make 2, 1 each with 3 strands of Color A and 3 strands of Color B.

1. Using 3 strands held together, cast on 4 stitches.

2. Work in Plain Stitch for 45 rows or until work measures 95" (241.5cm) or desired length. Bind off.

KNOTTED STITCH STRIP
1. Using 3 strands of Color C held together, cast on 4 stitches.

2. Work in Knotted Stitch for 45 rows or until work measures 95" (241.5cm) or desired length. Bind off.

Pom-Poms

1. Make six 5" (12.5cm)-diameter pom-poms, 2 in each color, as shown on page 17.

Assembly

1. Place 3 strips side by side with Color C strip in the middle.

2. Measure 12" (30.5cm) from end of strips. Using a 24" (61cm) length of Color C, tie an overhand knot around all 3 strips at the 12" (30.5cm) mark. Wrap the yarn around the strips several times. Tie ends together in an overhand knot and tuck them behind the wrap to hide them.

3. Braid the strips until 12" (30.5cm) remain unbraided. Repeat process in step 2 to tie other end of strips together.

4. Sew or tie a pom-pom to the end of each strip, matching the colors.

5. Weave in ends.

Yarn
The project shown uses Lion Brand® Yarn Hometown USA® (5oz./81yd. [142g/74m]), 3 skeins each #400S Neon Pink (Color A), #410S Neon Orange (Color B), #150 Chicago Charcoal (Color C).

Striped Knotted Stitch Capelet

Bundled up in this short cape, you'll be happy to venture out into any winter wonderland! The bold black and white stripes, Knotted Stitch, and metallic threads woven through the yarn give this piece a classy look that will make you want to wear it for every special occasion.

DIFFICULTY:

APPROXIMATE LENGTH:
42" (106.5cm)

APPROXIMATE WIDTH:
20" (51cm)

STRANDS:
Use 5 strands held together throughout

MATERIALS:
- 10 skeins super bulky weight yarn, 2 colors with metallic, 5 skeins each color
- 1 button (1½" [38mm])
- Sewing needle and coordinating thread

Alternative Closure

Don't feel like sewing on buttons? Use a pretty jewelry piece or a decorative shawl stick as a closure instead.

Capelet

1. Using 5 strands of Color A held together, cast on 7 stitches.

2. Work in Knotted Stitch for 46 rows, using the Horizontal Stripes technique on page 12 to change colors after every 2 rows. Work the two-tone stitch at the edge with the working yarn of both Color A and Color B held together as shown on page 12. Bind off using Color A.

Neckline

1. Cut 5 strands of Color A 40" (101.5cm) long for neckline.

2. Lay piece flat with short edges oriented vertically to your right and left and two-tone stitches along the bottom.

3. Weave neckline strands through stitches along the top edge (the edge without the two-tone stitches) as shown on page 15.

4. Slide stitches along neckline strands until top edge measures 25" (63.5cm) or desired length.

5. Finish both ends of neckline by tying strands together in an overhand knot over the end stitch. Weave in ends.

Finishing

1. Sew button to left side of neckline.

2. Weave in remaining ends.

Yarn

The project shown uses Lion Brand® Yarn Wool-Ease® Thick & Quick® (6oz./106yd. [170g/97m]), 5 skeins each #303 Constellation (Color A), #301 Celebration (Color B), and Blumenthal Lansing Cut-Outs 1½" (38mm) button, style #2410.

Two Layer Cape

With double the layers, this cape has double the drama! Use this pattern with different types of yarn to change up the look. Super bulky yarn will make a chunky, warm cape for cold weather, while lighter weight yarn will make a thin wrap suitable for springtime or cool summer nights.

DIFFICULTY:

APPROXIMATE LENGTH:
40" (101.5cm)

APPROXIMATE WIDTH:
32" (81cm)

STRANDS:
Use 6 strands held together throughout

MATERIALS:
- 6 skeins bulky weight yarn, 1 color
- 1 faux tortoiseshell button (2" [50mm])
- Tapestry needle

Alternative Closure

Don't feel like sewing on buttons? Use a pretty jewelry piece or a decorative shawl stick as a closure instead.

Cape

1. Using 6 strands held together, cast on 14 stitches.

2. Work in Twisted Stitch for 35 rows. Bind off.

Neckline

1. Cut 6 strands of yarn 36" (91.5cm) long for neckline.

2. Lay piece flat with short edges oriented vertically to your right and left.

3. Weave neckline strands through fifth stitch from top edge in each column (see page 15).

4. Slide stitches along neckline strands until top edge measures 18" (45.5cm) or desired length.

5. Finish both ends of neckline by tying strands together in an overhand knot over the end stitch. Weave in ends.

Finishing

1. Sew button to left side of neckline.

2. Weave in remaining ends.

Yarn
The project shown uses Lion Brand® Yarn Homespun®
(6oz./185yd. [170g/169m]), 6 skeins #329 Waterfall, and
La Mode 2" (50mm) button, style #29897.

One Point Wrap

Using a simple decrease technique, you can turn a basic wrap into something a little more unique. With one pointed end and buttons for a closure, this wrap makes the perfect addition to any outfit!

DIFFICULTY:

APPROXIMATE LENGTH:
46" (117cm), to point

STRANDS:
Use 5 strands held together throughout

MATERIALS:
- 5 skeins super bulky weight yarn, 1 color
- 3 ceramic buttons (1½" [4cm])

Alternative Closure
Don't feel like sewing on buttons? Use a pretty jewelry piece or a decorative shawl stick as a closure instead.

Yarn
The project shown uses Lion Brand® Yarn Wool-Ease® Thick & Quick® (6oz./106yd. [170g/97m]), 5 skeins #1351 Spice, and La Mode Textures 1½" (4cm) buttons, style #1059.

Wrap

1. Using 5 strands held together, cast on 7 stitches.

2. Work in Plain Stitch for 15 rows.

DECREASE SECTION

Row 1: Decrease 1 at start of row as shown on page 14.

Row 2: Decrease 1 at end of row.

Rows 3–6: Repeat Rows 1–2 once, then repeat Row 1 once more.

Row 7: Work last 2 stitches together, acting as both a decrease and a bind-off.

Finishing

1. Arrange buttons on flat edge of wrap as shown in photo and sew on using a strand of yarn.

2. Weave in all ends.

Shaped Shawl

Rectangles are not the only shape you can make in arm knitting! A simple increase and decrease technique allows you to make a triangle shape, perfect for a shawl or wrap.

DIFFICULTY:

APPROXIMATE LENGTH:
76" (193cm)

APPROXIMATE WIDTH:
36" (91.5cm)

STRANDS:
Use 5 strands held together throughout

MATERIALS
- 5 skeins bulky weight yarn, 1 color

Shawl

Using 5 strands held together, cast on 2 stitches.

Row 1: Work in Plain Stitch.

Row 2: Increase 1 (see page 13). Work all stitches in Plain Stitch (3 stitches).

Row 3: Work in Plain Stitch.

Row 4: Increase 1. Work all stitches in Plain Stitch (4 stitches).

Rows 5–21: Repeat Rows 3 and 4 for pattern 8 times, then repeat Row 3 once more (12 stitches). Work will be on your left arm.

Row 22: Decrease 1 (see page 14). Work remaining stitches in Plain Stitch (11 stitches).

Row 23: Work in Plain Stitch.

Repeat Rows 22 and 23 for pattern until 2 stitches remain. Bind off.

Weave in ends.

Tip

To make a larger shawl, continue the increase rows until you reach the height you desire. If you add increase rows, don't stress about decreasing. No matter how many rows you increase, to decrease simply repeat Rows 22 and 23 until you have two stitches remaining. Then bind off and weave in the ends.

Yarn

The project shown uses Lion Brand® Yarn Homespun®
(6oz./185yd. [170g/169m]), 5 skeins #415 Pesto.

Project Index

About the Author

Mary Beth Temple is an author/designer of both knitting and crochet patterns. Her work appears frequently in knitting and crochet magazines, including *Knit Simple, Vogue Knitting Crochet, Interweave Crochet, The Knitter* (UK), and *Inside Crochet* (UK). She is also the owner and lead designer for the popular pattern line *Hooked for Life*, which is available both online and in independent yarn stores.

Mary Beth is the author of the humor books *The Secret Language of Knitters* and *Hooked for Life: Adventures of a Crochet Zealot*. She has designed eight booklets—*DIY (Design it Yourself) Afghans, The Perfect Pillow: Ten Designs for Every Space, Easy Crochet Cowls, Handy Pocket Scarves, 25 Fun Dishcloths to Crochet, Tunisian Techniques: It's Easy to Crochet with Color, Arm Knitting*, and an upcoming title on finger knitting. Her most recent long-format book is *Curvy Girl Crochet: 25 Patterns that Fit and Flatter.*

Mary Beth can be found teaching at a wide variety of trade shows, conferences, and yarn stores.

Visit her online at *www.arm-knitting.com* and *www.hookedforlifepublishing.com.*